GRIEVANCES

By Thomas McKeon

Illustrations and Cover Art:
Colm McKeon

Printed in the United States of America
First Printing, 2016

ISBN: 978-0-9982449-0-7
Library of Congress Control Number: 2016917151

Published By:

NarrowBack Productions
San Francisco, CA USA
http://www.narrowbackproductions.com/

ACKNOWLEDGMENTS

Susan, Brian, Michael & Joseph for always showing me the bright side.

My parents and brothers for providing a decent training ground for storytelling, sarcasm, shit-talking and self-deprecation.

Colm McKeon for the hilarious illustrations and what I hope will be the relaunch of our highly lucrative movie production partnership.

Tim Reardon for his proofreading efforts but also for his advice and encouragement. It almost makes up for the time he crashed his makeshift go-cart and tore my Achilles Tendon back in the 7th grade. Almost.

INTRODUCTION

For the past several years, in December, I've posted a list of rants called "The Festivus 'Airing of Grievances' Project." The idea started when a coworker started posting three positive thoughts online each day, and was admittedly running out of ideas, when another coworker bet me that I couldn't post at least three negative thoughts each day. I did and referenced Festivus after one of my favorite "Seinfeld" episodes. Many seemed to enjoy the posts while others joined my suicide watch. Each year since, people have asked for more so it's become kind of a painful, anti-holiday tradition.

This book is a compilation of some of those rants, with a few new ones added as I'm not quite right with the world.

If just *one* person gets just a little something out of this book, then of course I would consider it to be an abysmal failure. Hey, I need to move some units here people.

-Thomas

Things that bug the living shit out of me, no matter how silly or small.

****

How about the Local Nightly News doing away with the stupid teasers?: "Who's trying to kill your children while you sleep?… Tune in at Eleven."

****

Medical Science Headlines: "Dramatic breakthrough in genetic research to cure xxx …. but it's a first step and we're at least 50 years away from human trials. To those people who read this article because a loved one is afflicted with the disease in the headline, forget we even mentioned it.

****

On Facebook, It's OK to just click the "Like" button or just enjoy from afar and not have to add the perfunctory "So Cute" comment to photos of pets or children or children with pets. Not casting aspersions, we've (meaning: women) have all done it.

Cool guys who insist on always backing into a parking spot. Known to some as "Fancy Parkers," they justify the 3x-time-wasting parking maneuver as saving time when pulling out. The only people who need a quick out are firetrucks and get-away cars.

****

24-Hr Cable News: They don't have enough content but they still need to fill the space. "Again, if you're just joining us, there is a hostage situation at a Tulsa McDonalds where somewhere between 1 and 53 people are being held at gun and/or knifepoint by a man, or group of men or a gaggle of women. It is unclear what the demands are at this time but let's turn to Suze Orman to get her reaction on the possible financial implications for those inside." I envision the producer off-camera constantly making the "stretch-it-out" motion, like pulling imaginary taffy, to keep the host talking until real facts come in.

****

People rooting through my recycling bin I've put out for the city to collect. Not sure why is bothers me so much, a general issue of fairness I guess, but the fact that this bothers me is another problem I have with the whole thing.

****

Walking face first into a spider web: Not only the creepy factor, but always sends me into a rage. Seems to happen to me at least once a week. Maybe I should clean up the place more often...or move out of the Munster mansion.

****

People who honk in tunnels for the fun: Hey, I remember my first time in a motor vehicle as well, Rainman.

****

House Hunting TV Shows: People in other areas of the country saying "It's a little bit smaller than what we were looking for" while staring at a 6500 sq. ft. palace on a couple of acres of land for $128K.

****

Walnuts: The bane of the nut world. Worse yet, unsalted walnuts. You can stuff them into a dense, rich brownie and you still can't get rid of the number-2-pencil-tasting effect of the dreaded walnut. At least have the decency to glaze & candy the crap out of them or coat them in enough salt to preserve them into the next century.

****

Changes in the Catholic mass: They say the changes are a better interpretation of the Latin, but with the extent of the changes, the guy who did the original translation must have been a complete buffoon. As I hear the crowd recite these still-foreign words, I feel like I'm on vacation in the mid-west and could only find a New Age church to keep up church-going appearances for the kids. Although, I'm pretty sure I'd have raged against Vatican II (Electric Boogaloo) back in the day as well. At least they didn't change the Hail Mary or the Our Father, else the Rosary would stumble right up to the funeral.

****

TV newscasters and their weird, fake TV voice with the head movements and nods. I'll bet he's a good guy but if I met Stone Phillips at a cocktail party, I'm pretty sure I'd have him in a headlock by the end of the night.

****

Lifetime Channel: Always "one woman's struggle" against the tyranny of men.

****

Wedding Seating Chart Organizers who insist on placing you with people you don't know: You know, to shake it up. "Hey, you know who would really hit it off? Tom and Tibor, the foreign exchange student!" Are you Julie McCoy, my Cruise Director? I don't want to meet anyone new and if I do it will be on my terms, which means someone I've casually known for at least 20 years if not known since kindergarten, and the relationship was cemented during a wild bachelor party, or at an after-sport drinking session or a shared near-death experience. Preferably all three.

****

Sports Parents: People living vicariously through their kids who give the coaches and referees the hardest time were probably not athletes growing up and don't understand the game. Chill. It's just a game. It would be better for you, your kid, the school and society at large if you lived vicariously through them in academics and/or community service.

****

Caillou: Every time I hear that deranged Charlie-Brown-lookin' kid giggle I want to go on a killing rampage.

****

Politician speak: Always short on the HOW. "What we NEED to do is improve the ECONOMY!" Ah, no wonder my "Economy…eShmonomy" platform didn't poll well in the blue or red states.

****

House Hunting TV Shows and "Entertaining:" They all talk about how the house is or is not suited for entertaining. "I like to be able to chat with my guests as I'm turning a goat on the spit in the kitchen." Really, how often does one entertain? I only entertain under protest. The worst shows are the international house hunting shows where the final scene is new homeowner awkwardly "entertaining" people that there is no way they know, having just moved to a foreign country. I'm pretty sure it's the TV crew, the gardener and some local homeless.

****

Junkmail disguised as a personal letter or an important notice from local, state or federal government. Even if it's something I want or need, I'll rip it up just because I think it's a shifty way to do business and marketers shouldn't be rewarded by such tactics. "Hey, I got a letter. What the?" [Rip!]

****

People who wait in a line of traffic and then get up to the toll booth only to then realize they need to pay a toll. "What, is there some sort of currency exchange required before I'm allowed to pass? Gee, maybe I have a $100 bill or some Spanish Doubloons in my trunk, if you'll hold on just a second…"

****

Telemarketers: Calls always come in during dinner or while putting the kids to bed. [Ring, Ring]…"Hello?"….First a pause…then a click and then…"Hello, Mr…MaKennon? How are ya doin' today sir?" If there is ever a time for the kids to learn curse words from me it's in this involuntary, Tourette-ian-like moment. "Go F$ck Yourself!" [slam!] "Who was that, Dad?" Recovering, then deflecting "Ah…it was Santa…I doubt he's coming now." "BWaaaaahh!"

****

People who will circle a parking lot for many minutes to get maybe a half dozen spots closer to their destination. Park and walk a little, tubby.

****

I like New Balance shoes but why do they need to make their shoelaces so damn long? Am I supposed to crisscross tie them up my calf like a Roman Centurion? To keep from stepping on them I have to quadruple tie them which then looks like a little shoelace bouquet on each foot. And forget about that old schoolyard bully trick of tying someone's shoes together by the laces and flinging them up around a telephone wire. These laces are so long the shoes would just dangle back down at eye level. Maybe their lace length is an anti-bullying measure? That is the only possible reason for it so I withdraw my complaint.

****

People paving over their lawns for the purpose of parking their cars on the sidewalk. "They paved paradise to put up a parking lot."

****

Public Restrooms: Not saying they have to be spotless but I think some people go out of their way to screw it up for the next person. Lift the seat BEFORE going #1 or at least wipe it afterwards. Hey Trigger, how about actually flushing before going back to your trough of food? Sometimes there is unknown organic material strewn all over and you'd swear someone birthed a calf in the stall just moments before you got there. And from my casual observations, many cowboys don't wash their hands after handling said calf.

****

The Facebook newbie: People who put a NEW post on their own wall as an in-no-way-connected response to a conversation or posting on someone else's site. "Ha ha…you are so right Terry! Are we still on for Thursday?" [cricket…cricket]

****

Shampoo bottles: Instructions always say "Rinse and Repeat." Would you buy dish liquid or laundry detergent that said the same thing? And ALL shampoo bottles say it – that's collusion! Why not add "and squeeze the rest of the bottle down the drain and buy more" to the label?

****

When you go to a class or seminar and first few hours are wasted on "Let's go around the room and introduce yourself, tell us what your interests are and what you'd like to get out of this course?" This isn't the Dating Game, get on with the class. "Hi I'm Thomas and I'm only interested in is getting this goddamn class started!" [Sound of screeching chairs as they shuffle a few inches away from me in all directions] I wonder if there is a class that teaches using introductions to waste time and if so, do they start that class off with introductions? Ah…I think I just blew your mind.

****

Every smarmy teenage actor on Nickelodeon and Disney channels: While not actually musicians, I'm sure each of them are getting ready to "drop" their own album.

****

People who go into independently owned stores and stock up only on sale items. I mean, carts full of the same sale item. Sales are to get people in to buy other things so seeing this kinda bums me out. And I'm sure most of these folks don't shop there regularly. At least buy a pack of gum, man. One that isn't on sale, that is.

****

Stuck in a long line of traffic with nowhere to go and people behind you start honking. It's like they can only see the car directly in front of them. [Honk! Honk!] "Ah, I don't know why you're just sitting there but I'd like to get in FRONT of you now. Thank you" [Honk! Honk!]

****

The House Hunting TV Show Flip Flop: Husband: "I like house x." Wife: "Well, I like house y." [Commercial break] Husband: "We've decided on... house y! It's our dream house and has everything we've ever wanted." It's OK buddy, I understand.

****

Flush Sensor on public toilets: I'm hardly a luddite when it comes to advances in bathroom technology. My sublime tech toilet experience in Tokyo was well documented in certain circles. But they have to improve the sensitivity of those auto-toilet flushing sensors. I put a seat cover on, turn around to start my hurried unbuckling routine en route to a seated positon and the toilet flushes before I can get there, sucking the seat cover down and spitting droplets of suspect water all over the seat. And after successfully sitting down on the seat cover, don't lean forward unless you want a startling, mini-bidet experience. So I'm forced to lean back, and to the left. Back, and to the left. I can't get any reading done that way.

****

Vitamin x is good for you; [10 Years later] Vitamin x causes cancer; [15 years later] Some Vitamin x is good for some people some of the time...maybe...if you're French.

****

When Facebook or other social media service changes something, your life is not over. Deep breath. It's a free service you are not required to use. Adapt or move on.

****

People stealing donations we leave out for local charities of the disabled. Karma, dispatch them quickly and with extreme prejudice.

****

80s-90s Sitcoms: Every show has a fat, stupid husband and a hot, mean-spirited wife who always catches him doing something wrong. The reality is that sometimes the hot wife doesn't catch the husband.

****

Movie "reboots" as they're called now: Not a remake but a different story, actors and characters from a movie of the same name but trying to capitalize on the success of the original. The newer "Karate Kid" was about a kid learning Kung Fu. I think I'll make a movie about a trade embargo and call it "Star Wars." Oh wait, that *was* Star Wars: Episode 1

****

Can't they do something with the awkward pause when interviewing someone via satellite? I'm sure they can insert delays and edits in semi-realtime to make the conversation flow. Hell, why not pre-tape and edit it? Do we really miss something if it's not live? If I was the producer I'd have newscaster ask the next question immediately to make the interviewee come off as disheveled if not evasive.

****

Packaging on kids toys, vacuum forming plastic: I first try to pull it apart by hand, then slice it with my car keys, then jab it with scissors to finally get a finger in to repeat step one. I then apply a tourniquet before I pass out from all the blood loss.

****

Packaging on kids toys, Twisty Ties: These are the little bastards that secure the toy to the inside of the packaging. For some reason there needs to be thousands of them, twisted dozens of times each to tie down important items like Tickle Me Elmo. I don't think the Enola Gay went to this much trouble to secure its cargo. My hands will be cramping into the new year.

****

This has happened to me several times since becoming a father: I'm out somewhere with my kids and without my wife and someone, always a female for some reason, refers to this act as "babysitting." "Oh, I see you got stuck babysitting!" as she nervously looks over my kids as if they could have possibly developed rickets in the few short hours that I've been alone with them. Babysitting? I'm pretty sure these are my kids and I'm not getting $15 an hour so I would classify it as "attempted parenting."

****

Unsalted butter: Unless we're baking, and I don't bake, you can keep it away from me. Salt is the most of the flavor and the butter provides the texture. French bread and baked potatoes are the preferred butter conveyances.

****

I know I should suspend disbelief, especially for superhero movies, but in all depictions of the Hulk's transformation, his shirt rips apart but his pants grow with his size. Even when he grows bigger than a house his pants fit properly. I could use pants like that for the holidays.

****

News always focuses on the negative. If it bleeds it leads, I guess. Not that they need to be Pollyanna about the world but how about a balance of stories that don't make me lose faith in humanity on a daily basis? Thank you.

****

I don't like unscripted TV shows. They give people the opportunity to embarrass themselves, and they often do. All reality TV shows (sure they are semi-scripted but not scripted enough), award shows and game shows. I even have difficulty with standup comedy, unless it's a really honed show or was recorded and edited just for the highlights. Just stick to the script please.

****

I find this to be an issue mainly with newbies in electronic communication but the PEOPLE WHO WRITE EVERYTHING IN ALL CAPS REALLY STRESSES ME OUT. Maybe it's because I had an old boss that used to actually "yell" this way in email. I think spelling & grammar checkers in applications should add an "All Caps Check" to their list of suggestions: "Did you really mean to wail like a banshee?"

****

I can understand the occasional mistake, especially when responding via smart phone, but there are some folks who consistently "Reply All" to corporate-wide emails. Is it attention seeking or someone just not clear on simple email concepts? Dunno. Don't care. Stop.

[Subject: Re: Company Blood Drive | To: Company-All]
"Hi Tina, Can you still give blood if you have Hep C?"

****

Top 40 Radio Announcers, with their fake radio voices, talking over the entire intro of a song and stop just before the vocals come in. Hey, you hit the post...that's really cool man! Now, how about a Long Distance Dedication to "shut your trap and let us listen to the music?"

****

America's Funniest Home Video (AFV) is one of my kids' favorite shows but they may as well rename it "America's Fathers Getting Whacked in the Crotch (AFWC)." Every show you'll see some unsuspecting male, minding his own business in the corner of the TV screen holding a rope to a piñata, and on the other side of the screen some sugared-up kid spinning around like the Tasmanian Devil with a baseball bat. You know what happens next. I've seen it so often on this show that after the first two frames of a scene and I know instantly which blunt object is going hit whose nether region. When I watch my own home videos I half expect an errant fungo to come spinning into the frame and nail me in the tenders. Which reminds me, I need a new cup.

****

From random people you meet on the street, to people you sorta know, to colleagues at work, to everyone in civilized society, if someone says "hello" to you, muster the energy to respond in kind. At least make eye contact and give a nod. It amazes me the number of times people won't even look up, let alone give some response to a pleasantry. Get up really early on a Sunday, when the elderly rule the streets, and go out to a grocery store or a coffee shop and you'll experience how it's supposed to be.

****

When I hear any song on the radio from either Steely Dan or Supertramp, I have to use all of my power not to turn my vehicle into oncoming traffic.

****

The Pre-game shows on Super Bowl Sunday: Mindless. Endless. How many times can you hear the meat-headed, sausage-fingered announcers say "What they need to do is convert on 3rd down" in a broadcast? Isn't' that true of all games, Tank? "What they need to do is score more points than the other team to win this game." I can watch those NFL films all day, though, so they should just keep running those up until kickoff and at halftime. Actually, I want the guy who narrates those to narrate the film of my life that will be played at my funeral. My funeral will of course be MC'd by Morgan Freeman and there will be the obligatory Blue Angels flyover to the strains of "Rock You Like a Hurricane" as one jet peels off, missing man formation, over The Sunset. Ah, what was I talking about again?

****

Circuses: Specifically, the animals and how they are manipulated, kinda bum me out. On the oppression-depression scale, the circus is one small step below the zoo and one step above a cock fight.

****

Memory Foam mattresses with amnesia: I've been trust falling back into an ever-deepening tempur crater each night for the better part of 5 years. In the morning I'm stuck like a physically-stunning Greek statue impressed in its custom-cut, protective foam shipping container.

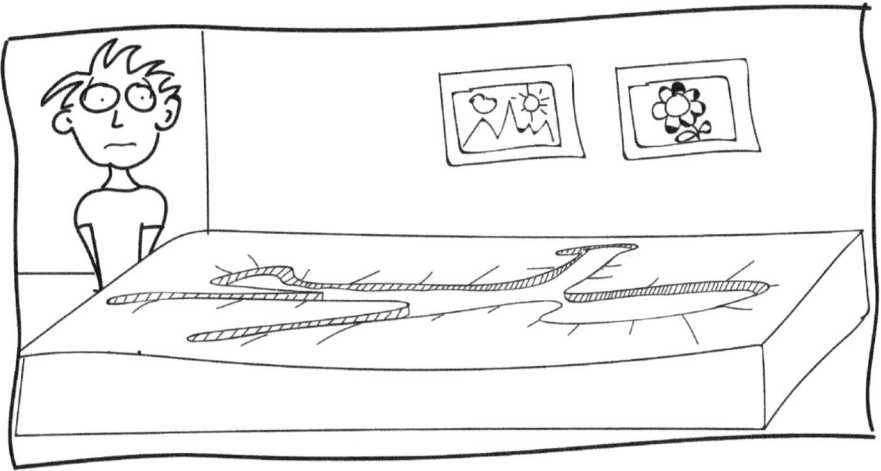

****

Giving Directions to non-natives: Being a San Francisco native, and living in a cocoon most of my life, I have to admit I know little about The City. Sure, I know some of the main streets but my directions are based on old attractions and sites (in my 20s-30s it was bars) because I don't know street names, which is of no help to non-natives. "Go up Geary and past the Coronet (no longer there) and just before Sears (now a Best Buy, I think)." I barely know the neighborhood names aside from The Sunset, the Parkside, the Richmond, North Beach and Noe Valley. Everything else is "downtown." "It's over by Goodman's Lumber" or "right before the Cow Palace" or "down the block from Tower Records towards the pyramid" are common, useless utterances. I usually just taper off and defer to someone who just moved to the city.

****

When traveling abroad and you meet people "from San Francisco:"
- Me: "Oh really? What part of The City are you from?"
- Guy: "Hayward"
- Me: "Ah…is that near Goodman's Lumber?"

****

People in the grocery express lane with too many items: The sign should read "15 items or less & 90 IQ or more" Maybe stores can develop a conveyer belt that will eject contents when drool-covered groceries are detected.

****

The overuse of "[sic]" in the media these days: I'm sure it's due to increased celebrity activity on social media but I now seem to see this editorial comment daily. I can understand occasionally using it within one's own written word, as in "I really meant that" but inserting it into another's quote, to me, seems a) Unnecessary: If it's in quotes, we'll take your word for it that it's a direct quote, spelling & grammar issues included, and b) Very snobby: It's a reporter's way of motioning with their thumb and rolling their eyes as they say "Get a load of this simpleton!" Oh, Mr. Entertainment Reporter, you are so, so clever. We worship you on high.

****

There are parking spots labeled for compact cars so there should also be spots designated for full-sized vehicles only. I want to throw a justified sneer to just one Prius owner before I die.

****

San Francisco Board of Supervisors: We should ban all non-binding votes. "We're against Happy Meals in Afghanistan" It does nothing but waste our taxpayer money and reaffirms SF as nut-bag west, and I'm a (friend-accused) liberal.

****

These days most people wouldn't toss an aluminum can out of a car window or slam an apple core down on the sidewalk before entering a building, but somehow its considered acceptable behavior to many to flick a cigarette butt wherever-the-frig they want. It's not only disgusting litter but it's still on fire! I assume there was no training for this at peer pressure camp but it is so prevalent the world over that it must be innate human behavior. My neighbor drops butts all over the sidewalk and in my driveway as if it's his God-given right. I think I'll take up smoking giant bags of flaming Irish Wolfhound shit and leave them on his doorstep. Hey man, I'm addicted.

****

I'm OK with "sharing the road" and there are probably more inconsiderate drivers than bicyclists, but I get a bit annoyed by bicyclists who ride in the middle of the street with rest of traffic rather than in the designated bike lane. "Woohoo! I'm as fast as a car!" Ah, no you're not. Move to the side.

****

I'm not a coffee snob by any means but Starbucks coffee is just bitter battery acid. I really want to like it. I like the stores, located everywhere, with their soothing adult-contemporary music and inviting, cozy decor. And the people working there always seem friendly and happy. Yet, every time I drink their coffee, I get a look on my face like I'm chewing on a wasp and I end up buckling over with massive cramping, desperately begging passers-by for an epidural until I eventually collapse to my knees in agony, eyes cocked skyward and arms stretched out wide, as I shriek out to the heavens "My God, My God, why have you forsaken me?!" You know, as I read this back, I think I just have an ulcer.

****

I hate any movie, TV show or commercial where animated creatures sing pop songs and/or rap. I just about plunged an ice pick through my ear drums during a screening of "Happy Feet." Actually, I still may, just at the thought of that movie.

At the beginning of the stop-motion classic "Santa Claus is Coming to Town," Kris Kringle and the elves pronounce the family matriarch's name as "Tawn-ta" but when Kris is older, and Hollywood legend Mickey Rooney takes over the voice, he pronounces her name "Tan-ta." I'm sure the producers were too afraid to correct Mr. Rooney and we are forever stuck with this blatant disregard for continuity. Jules Bass and/or Arthur Rankin Jr: Each year we are all reminded of your cowardice and we will never forgive you. Never!

Drivers who are too cool to use their turn signals.

****

Seems like every time I go to a concert, just as the band comes on, some clown lifts a girl on his shoulders right in front of me. Every time. As if seeing that balancing/courting act is why I paid the $150. If I ever need to meet someone at a concert I say "look for a wiry, shirtless male with Teeth-By-Meth™ that has a not-so-wiry female, sporting a tank top and tramp stamp, teetering on his shoulders, dousing the crowd with her beer and shouting "F*ck yeah! Metalicaaaaa!" (at a U2 concert) and I'll be directly behind them." I'm waiting for it to happen to me at the movie theater. Meth Man with Ms. Tramp-a-Stamp on his shoulders and a thankfully-unstamped kid in her arms spilling popcorn all over and she's shouting "F*ck yeah! Arial!" (at a "Frozen" matinee) as my kids, oblivious to the scene, wrench their necks to see the screen.

****

Toy Racetrack Commercials: Deceptive advertising at its peak. Cranked up music, explosions, lasers, WWE-like announcer taunting as the car jumps off the track, flipping end-over-end through a ring of fire, landing back on the track just in front of the other car and dashing across the finish line and the kids jump up into a freeze-frame high five as the music crescendos. Compare that to reality: No music. No announcer. No fire rings. If you dare go full throttle, the car instantly shoots off the track and rolls under the bed. You eventually end up dialing back on the throttle and the cars go slowly but steadily around the loop, with that hypnotic swishing sound. The kids get bored within 5 minutes and jam the track under the bed, never to be played with again. There must be twenty odd miles of track under those beds by now. But, rest assured, next Christmas we'll see another commercial and buy another track. That's just the way it is. It's too late for me–I realize that now–but with some psychotherapy and God's tender mercies, maybe my kids can break this vicious cycle with their own children.

****

Conference/Classroom Repeaters: People who pretend to participate by merely repeating what the instructor says during a lecture.
- Teacher: "The answer is 3."
- Kiss-ass: "So, what you're saying, Professor, if I may, is that the answer is unequivocally 3? Oh, I see, I see. That is quite an interesting dichotomy."

****

People who think I bought a truck in order to help them move. I bought it to get...to meet...Ah, who am I kidding? Who needs something hauled to the dumps this weekend?

****

3D movies: Twice the price, gimmicky FX and my youngest kid refuses to wear the glasses, watching a blurry movie in between his 10 trips to the bathroom. Instead of watching the movie I find myself watching my kid and I get increasingly more anxious as his eyes slowly cross, and then I need to go to the bathroom.

****

They say if you love what you do then you'll never work a day in your life. Well, I've been working every friggin' second for the last 25+ years.

****

It still bugs me that NBC station in Bay Area is now out of San Jose. Even though they've taken a few familiar folks from other local news staffs it still feels like I'm watching news out of Redding or something.

****

Charlie Brown Christmas tree: It's always bothered me that the tree Charlie Brown picked out was all bare and branchy but when the gang fixes it up, with a flurry of arms and ornaments, it's suddenly full and festive. I don't think it's the same tree. It's obvious to me now they swapped out the tree using some kind of animation trickery but freezing the DVD down frame by frame I still can't see how they pulled off the switch. The point, I thought, that there was beauty in the gangly tree and not that they can make it look good & normal with enough tinsel and ornaments. What kind of message does that send to the nation's trees?

****

People smoking in car in front of you: Your car can be hermetically sealed and the smell is still going to get in within seconds. Makes me want to pull in front of that car and release a smell of my own, but I fear the resulting dead livestock on the side of the road would lead to widespread panic and frantic trips to Devil's Tower.

32

****

Pants: Nice days, rainy days, snowy days: Every day is shorts day in my opinion. My sole goal left in life is to never have to wear long pants again. Some say I've given up. But to truly give up, one needs to move onto sweatpants. That's in my 10-year plan.

****

Jägermeister: Oh dark, vile seepage from Hell's septic tank, what havoc you hath wrought lo these many years. Faces—nay, the fabric of space-time itself—disfigure from a mere molecule of your wretched stench. I curse you in the name of all that is holy.

****

When politicians feign outrage at any misstep made by the opposing side, no matter how small. "Perhaps the good Senator from Illinois would care to explain why his car did not come to a complete stop at that stop sign on the corner of Grant and Main last Thursday afternoon. If he doesn't follow the rules of the road, who knows what OTHER rules he's bending. The American people deserve an answer!" Politicians have to be thick-skinned to reach office so the "outrage charade" they put on just to drum up controversy is insulting to both sides and a huge time waster.

****

People who leave mattresses and other junk on the street corner, expecting someone will eventually get disgusted and pick it up, which they eventually will. Even more insulting is when they leave a "free" sign on it, as if they are doing someone a favor. And most of those mattresses aren't very comfortable.

****

In every city, and even a TV show name, the department is called "Parks and Recreation (Park & Rec)" but in San Francisco it was somehow switched to "Recreation and Parks (Rec & Park)." I can't find out when or why this change occurred. Perhaps someone in the Rec department with a serious chip on their shoulder.

****

When women dance with their arms over the heads: A modern day Salome–sans severed, haloed head–to draw attention to themselves. "Hey, Look at me! Look at me!"

****

I've been commuting two hours a day for the better part of the 20 years, and in that time I've come to the conclusion that if you're male and you drive an Audi, you're probably an asshole. Just…probably.

****

The phrase "Let's take that offline:" I don't think anyone who has ever uttered that phrase in the history of conference calls has actually followed up "offline." And that's the point. I think we should be honest and replace the phrase with the chant "Tan-gent! Tan-gent!" and then go right on with the call.

****

When you are reintroduced to someone you've casually met before by a mutual friend: "Tom, you remember Sally?" "Yes, good to see you again." I say as a normal, non-confrontational transition from our mutual friend's opening. "No, we've never met before," Sally corrects, without hesitation or emotion. Would it kill you to say we've met, especially when someone says we have and I go along with it with my greeting? Or at least not address the prior meeting issue and just start with a simple "Hello?" Am I on trial for a heinous crime and you don't want to be accused of guilt by association or something? [Don't answer that]. One person I "know" has done this to me at least three times over the years, and after the last denial I could have sworn I heard a cock crow off in the distance.

****

Raccoons: A pack of them wander over from the lake every other night, tipping over garbage cans and spreading crud all over the place. I've set up lights to distract them and bungeed the cans shut but they still knock the cans over every week, just because. I know these animals are ballsy but they are now walking past people in the middle of the day to get to garbage cans at the lake, and couldn't give two shits about it. Whatever happened to "nocturnal?" What ever happened to "being afraid of humans?" Well, somebody's going to have to make these animals scared of us again, but it won't be me because I'm a big wuss. The kids are mortified when I let out "I hope that was one of ours. Take that ya bastard!" when I see one squashed on the side of the road.

****

Carts and Baskets at the grocery store: They are either not there or there with crud inside like a soiled tissue or scummy coupon page, or the cliché wobbly wheel. So I stumble through the store without a basket, balancing various grocery items on my person like the Baker on Sesame Street with all the pies, ready to topple. Here's a tip for store owners: Put a few of spare, clean hand baskets in the back center of the store to help stubborn people like me save a little face. And pies.

****

Incontinence and the top bunk.

THOMAS MCKEON
****

Carl's Jr commercials: You know the ones. Good looking people not eating, but smashing giant burgers into their faces, with sauce dripping all over their clothes. What response does sauce spilling on clothes get in real life? That's right, it's an "Ah Shit!" so why do they continually feature it in their commercials? And they must use models with small heads and hands because there is no way the burgers are that big in real life. (Or maybe they just make bigger burgers for the commercials? Yes, that would seem more likely.) The gorging act is so off-putting that it neutralizes the actors' good looks so they may as well stick any schlub in there to binge and purge in slow motion. And who watches these commercials and thinks to themselves "Oh, I'm gonna get me some of that right now. Gonna get messy. Messy all...night...long!" It's food porn. It's fast food porn. It's American fast food porn and Carl's Jr. seems to be shooting for the Hustler position in that market. The sloppy ad campaign has been going on for years so it must be working somewhere.

****

Graffiti: People always try to justify the illegal act as an "artistic expression" until it's done on the side of their own house. Often times it's a sloppy, hurried and often unintelligible "tag" that will take 10x the amount of time and thought to cover up than the time and thought it took to create it. My neighbor's car door was tagged last year. If that happened to me, it would literally & figuratively drive me mad.

Legos: It's crack for kids. My boys *must have* every Lego diorama they see. They put it together once and then it breaks apart a few days later, never to be whole again. Every midnight trek to the bathroom I must navigate these Danish landmines, spread all over the floor, by sweeping one leg in front of me, back and forth, like some sort of a breathtakingly-muscular metal detector. My latest hobby is toting the Legos out into the yard, a handful at a time, and dropping them through hole in my pocket and out my pantleg, Shawshank-style, as the kids eye me suspiciously from the window. By my calculations, I'll be Lego-free by Spring of 2028.

****

Decent computer printers are now under $100 but their ink cartridges cost at least that much, paid out every two months. And imagine what 3D printer "cartridges" will cost when they catch on. Forget drugs, we need a War on the Ink Cartels.

****

Basketball players, especially pro basketball players, who need to slap everyone's hand between free throws. Do they really need constant reassurance like that? What are they, aging Hollywood actresses? "Hey Shaq, we believe in you man…(side of the mouth) even though you just chucked that first free throw over the backboard."

****

Drivers in front of you who insist on looking at the person they are talking to in the passenger seat as they try to drive: Driving slowly, slight car sway onto the road braille each time they look at the passenger. I barely make eye contact with the people I'm talking to when I'm not driving.

****

Parking Meters: Furiously pumping coins into the meter as the ticking starts. Fumbling, eyes darting from palm to slot to meter to palm, sweat forming on my brow like I'm disarming a bomb or something. By the time I get to my last coin, the time on the meter has already run out.

****

Guys who use the word "sweet," as in "That was one sweet bike trail!"

****

The dozens of "subscribe" cards that magazine publishers insist on stuffing into each issue, dropping to the floor with every other page turn. If you subscribe to a magazine and it's delivered to your house, I think they should be subscription-card-free. I mean, I do most of my reading in the bathroom (dramatic pause) and I doubt any visitor would touch a magazine in there let alone stuff a card from it in their pocket on their way out.

****

When MC's/DJs use the following phrases: "At this time…" and/or "I'd like to…"As in "At this time, I'd like to introduce the couple of the hour, Mr. and Mrs. Anderson!" The crowd should then respond, "OK, go ahead and introduce them then." Both phrases are awkward attempts at formality and just meaningless filler. If it's "at this time" then just say it; If it's at some other time, then you can tip off the crowd. If "I'd like to" is really asking permission, then wait for permission to be granted, but if you are not asking permission then just do/say it. "At this time, I'd like to end this rant."

****

The "slippery slope" argument, often introduced with the phrase "the next thing you know…", used to justify any wild stretch an alarmist can conjure up. "If we let the government dictate the size of the soft drinks our kids can buy then the next thing you know, jackbooted government thugs will be raping kittens on the White House lawn!" Huh?

GRIEVANCES

****

The forced misuse of adjectives as adverbs: A very common one these days is "crazy" as in "she is crazy talented." What is this, an "advertive?" I'm even starting to see this bastardization used in reputable publications. If I was an editor I'd add a comma after every "crazy" until its use subsided. Then again, there is a long history of "advertive" usage in New England, as in "He is wicked smart." Humm, I don't want some wicked tough Southie to kick my ass. Well then, I amend my rant to be: I don't like "neo-advertive" usage by people who can't beat me up.

****

You always see it during the winter holidays at the mall: People who bust out their winter gear–scarves, gloves, boots, ear muffs, tuques, etc.– even when the weather is nice out. I get the whole festive seasonal garb thing but some overdue it to the point where you'd think they were summiting Everest. You usually spot them in the food court, holding a Starbucks, chatting to be seen and sweating profusely. There is always at least one guy wearing a perfectly-set-by-his-stylist Santa hat, going for that "girls will think I'm cute and whimsical" look that you want to smack off his head. If these people really dressed for the temperature in San Francisco, they'd be wearing these outfits in July.

GRIEVANCES

****

On afternoon talk shows when the camera cuts to people in the audience who constantly smile and nod in agreement as common sense advice spews out of the guest's mouth. Guest: "We should not light puppies on fire and toss them out onto freeways..." (Camera cuts to a tree-hugging Wiccan in third row as she open-mouth grins through exaggerated nods and slow claps, as if this earth-shattering "advice" is striking a unique chord with her).

****

Captcha: These are the skewed letters/numbers that you have to type in when submitting an online form to prove that you are indeed a person and not a computer. I think we're at the point where the humans asked to retype them can't even decipher the images being used but trolling code can, so maybe it's time to try something else.

****

People holding their cel phone in front of them as they drive like it's a friggin' Star Trek communicator: It's a hands-free law in California not an ear-free law. "But officer, I wasn't holding it to my ear...(with a subtle wave of the finger, the Jedi Mind Trick)...so there'll be no ticket for me today. Move along." [Yes, I realize that a Star Trek and Star Wars reference in the same rant may make some people angrier than Gandalf getting hit in the tenders with a snitch at a Quidditch match].

****

Streetcleaners: It's bad enough that they switched to a confusing every-other-week schedule to save money (actually, I believe The City lost money with this move because there are now fewer parking tickets) but the sweepers seem to do very little in terms of actually cleaning the streets. Their purpose seems to be making loud noise to agitate old folks and pets while spewing garbage up onto the sidewalk or into the middle of the street. They may as well use snow blowers to shoot the crap up onto my lawn more efficiently.

****

The Facebook Birthday app: Sure, I'll let you add me so an app automatically sends me a note on my birthday without your further involvement. Wow, you really shouldn't have!

****

Guys at PGA events who yell out "Get in the hole!" whenever a pro swings his club. I can just see the Bro-falling-around-laughing and the Bro-high-fiving and the Bro-chest-bumping routines after each completely original, perfectly timed utterance. Good one, Spalding. Wasn't it funny the first 10 million times? I can't wait to see the first Pro completely lose it and smash his driver off the skull of one of these tools.

****

Overuse of the word "profound:" I believe the "profound movement" started during Oprah's farewell season when she used the word on average of 189 times per episode. "This moisturizer touched me…in a…profound…way."

****

There are no "stories" anymore, everyone has a goddamn "narrative."

****

Articles come out every month or two about insomnia and how it leads to increased risk of depression, heart attack, cancer, etc. And they always end with the same sage advice "So get your sleep." Oh, is that all I need to do? Something other than grievance lists to pour over neurotically as I lie awake each night.

****

Password rules: Every website/company has a different policy. "They must be a minimum of 5 characters, with one capitol letter, one lower case character, one special character, one number and an umlaut. You cannot use a password used in the last 6 months. Passwords cannot contain your name, the company name or the name of anyone in your family going back 3 generations. Passwords must be changed every 32.5 minutes or your account will be locked. You have exceeded the number of attempts and your account is now locked. You'll now have to try to figure out how to contact the IT department to have your account unlocked when you can't even log into the IT help desk system to make the request because your account is locked. Goodbye."

****

Public hearing to "discuss" raising rates: Utilities, bridge tolls, school tuition etc. Has anyone in all of human history put forth an argument that actually changed managements' minds? Manager: "So, you're saying you'd be paying more outta pocket and that's not fair? Humm, I never looked at it that way. We withdraw our tuition increase proposal!" (Cheers as guy carried out on shoulder tops, shaking clasped hands to each side of his head in a self-laudatory fashion as "Hurrah!" chants echo back through the chamber, slowly trailing off as the jubilant crowd heads toward the town square to meet the mayor who's standing by with the key to the city.)

****

The uptalk speech pattern used by many American teenagers these days: It drives me, like, crazy?

****

Don't you hate it when the local TV news does a story on obesity and they play "B Roll" footage of "full bodied" people on the street–anonymous from-the-neck-down shots–and you recognize your snug, faded "Rocky (1)" gray sweat pants, flip-flops with off-white tube socks and the weathered '80s-era Niner jersey with the name "McKeon" stretched to the limit of still-recognizable letters on the back? Yeah, I hate when that happens too.

****

When women say "my girlfriend" about their platonic female friend: "Last night I went to a great new club with my girlfriend." Not sure when or why it started but many women seem to make this reference. Perhaps it started long ago as some sort of subtle relationship cue to avoid confrontation with current partner and/or put out signal to potential suitor and latter-day women just adapted it as a term of endearment? Not sure. Still, after many, many years of research–pouring over countless documents and hundreds of unanswered (per my lawyer: "non-creepy", "non-threatening") hand-delivered letters to Dear Abby–I have yet to trace its origins. I tried using "my boyfriend" the other day and, surprisingly, nobody just rolled with it like they do with women.

****

Free sample people at Costco: Not the causal shopper who happens upon a handout but the people who go there with the intent of eating a full meal. These people move from stand to stand like they're stations of the cross–throwing elbows, cart jockeying–all to get that last small cup filled with Wasa breadcrumbs. Less mobile versions of The Samplers stand at the pseudo stage, nodding with feigned interest or understanding at the guy rockin' the headset mic who's proselytizing about the virtues of a blender's triple blade and variable speeds, just waiting for the guy to shut his trap and start pouring out samples. The aisles are crowded enough as it is without this sorry lot of foragers adding to the congestion.

****

When marketing types refer to things, like software design, as "sexy." Sure, it's been a while for me but I don't think that's how it works.

****

Domain trolls, a.k.a Cybersquatters: These are people who buy up web domain names with no intention of using them but merely to sell them to the highest bidder. People naming a company these days often start with the domain name and when all the good ones are taken they start making words up, dropping vowels which is also quite annoying. Ah, but enough of my bellyaching. Today is a great day as I announce my new web consulting venture! Please visit us at:
http://www.DonkeySchlong68.net/

****

When scientists/doctors say "We're closer than we've ever been before" to solving an issue. What else are they supposed to say? "Well, I gotta admit…those last 5 years of intensive Coco Puff prostate cancer therapy really set us back. Wow, we really had our heads up our asses when we burned the research for all the other proven therapies. And now we're much, much further away from finding a cure than ever before."

****

You know, those crosswalk buttons and the close elevator door buttons are not hooked up to anything. It's a conspiracy perpetrated by the Illuminati, for reasons still opaque. Oh, you know what else is controlled by the Illuminati? Snopes.com. They created it in an attempt to discredit all the actual truths spewing out into cyberspace each day. Think about it: A website that attempts to discredit most everything else on the web? Who made them the final say on the internet? The Illuminati, that's who. You're welcome.

****

Garage sale people: Not your neighbor stopping by on their morning walk or the person that rubbernecks as they drive by before they pull over, I'm talking about the professional picker types who search out these domestic flea markets on the weekends. No matter what the price, these borderline carnies will always try to talk you down. "How much for the comic books?" "1 cent each." Slight pause. Head cocks to the side, fingers begin scratching chin, eyes narrowing like a sniper training on his target through the sights. "How about a ha'penny for ALL of them?" (Cue Motörhead's "Ace of Spades" cranked to "11" to accompany my strong-armed, profanity-laced shepherding of said carny down the driveway and out into the street.)

****

C&E Catholics: These are people who are only overwhelmed with "The Guilt" to go to church twice a year, on Christmas and Easter. They don't know the elaborate kneel-stand-sit routines nor the optimized flow paths to and from Communion; Always over-dressed, wearing bonnets and shit; and enthusiastically yet wrongly with the response "AND ALSO WITH (now looking around in confusion, tapering off) also with…you?" They crowd the aisles and stuff the pews so I can't get to my usual section/seat. I'm not going back to C&E masses until Monsignor assigns PSLs (Personal Seat Licenses).

****

On many golf courses, at least for me and my luck, the booze/snack cart seems to only circle the 9th green, which kinda defeats its purpose. "Hello, mythical cart person. Your cart is obviously tethered to the pro shop thus keeping you in this safe but confining orbit around the clubhouse. However, I'm happy to buy a drink from you now rather than from the snack bar which, at the moment, is closer to me than you are as you yell to get our attention. Oh, and I insist on giving you a huge tip for your efforts. Thanks and we'll see you again as we exit the 18th green."

****

When people say "Enjoy" when they had nothing to do with what you are about to enjoy. Not the normal, "I hope you enjoy yourself at the blah, blah blah." It's the one word, almost-a-command, usually in closing: "Enjoy!" It's like they are trying to take some credit for that thing or granting you some kind of permission. "Oh really, I can enjoy the vacation I paid for? That's very generous of you!"

****

Anytime two or more males of the human species get together socially some female throws out the "Male Bonding" label. How about we start labeling it when two or more women are out together? Since "Gossiping About The Mutual Friend Who Didn't Make It Out That Night" is too long we can just use "Pillow Fighting."

****

Cialis commercials where older couples are engaged in some random activity and then the guy gets that pervy look on his face. The woman always freezes with a slight "Oh shit!" panic and once she realizes he's seen her see him and there's no way out, she gives in with a slight giggle. In the real world, mature women learn to never make eye contact.

****

Diet Noise: Portion control. Eat more to weigh less. Skip a meal. You can't skip a meal or your metabolism will go awry. Wine and chocolate are good for you and so is coffee but only if you are paradoxically French. Eggs are good. Eggs are bad. Eggs are neither good nor bad. Carbs: good carbs, bad carbs, no carbs. Study: Thin people tend to drink more milk. Study: Milk is good for baby calves only. Diet soda has no calories. Diet soda confuses your body as if it does have calories so it goes into fat storage mode. Diet soda, with its fake sugar carcinogens, is worse than regular soda. Eat fruit. Don't eat fruit, it contains too much sugar. Sugar is bad. High Fructose Corn Syrup is the most evil substance in the universe. Sugar is good again, but only if it's extracted from Mexican Coca Cola. Olestra is the future of dieting. Olestra is the present of sharting. Eat more fish, but watch mercury levels. Eat veggies only, but take an iron supplement. Exercise, but check with your doctor first. Jim Fixx died of a heart attack while running. Eat protein only. Atkins may have died from heart disease. Butter is bad, margarine is good. Margarine is toxic, butter is good. Report: Happy people tend to be thinner. Retort: Thin people are happier because they aren't fat. Learn to accept yourself. No pain, no gain. No pain, no pain. All this typing is making me hungry.

****

I will not watch a show called "Finding Bigfoot" but would consider watching a show called "Found Bigfoot."

****

Video arcades are torture enough with kids but now they have these ones that spew out a couple of tickets at the end of the game so the kids can pick out a "prize" with their winnings. This ticket angle doubles the amount of time you spend there, which I guess is their goal. So I end up following the kids around for hours on end with a train of tickets dragging behind me, making sure to never mix them up or face a child's wrath, leading up to the final, tortuous stand at the prize counter staring at absolute junk. The poor person working there employs some kind of fuzzy math to move the kids along but it never seems to work as the kids, in the excitement, forget basic addition…and basic English for that matter. "How much tickets does I have? 15? OK I'll take that electric guitar on the top shelf….ah…the 5 foot SpongeBob doll…that remote control helicopter…two Xboxes…and…ah… I'll take the rest as a candy payout." [Worker's doll-eyed stare & the sound a single cricket chirping] The "prizes" they end up with are worth less than the money we'd get if we'd recycled the paper tickets. I think I'd pay double to go to an arcade that doesn't spit out those damn tickets.

****

Opt-out links in email that don't automatically opt you out when clicked: "Please fill out a page full of information about yourself so we can unsubscribe you and [ahem] never bother you again."

****

Those thick cardboard or mini-pamphlet ads in magazines that force the magazine to open to that page every time you pick it up. I even rip these out at the dentist's office.

****

Infomercials and their crazy deals: No matter how good they sound, you know there has to be a catch. "We'll send you not just one knife. Not just two knives. Not even… THREE …knives. We'll send you THREE HUNDRED (hundred…HUNdred…HUNDRED) knives! And, we'll throw in a free mountain bike! And if you call in the next 30 minutes, we'll throw in 35 acres of pristine real estate in beautiful California Pines. All for just $19.95! (speedily mumbled) You just pay shipping and handling." That sounds…too…good. Humm, not sure what "handling" actually entails but I'm guessing someone will be handling my credit card information for years to come.

****

People who loiter in coffee shops for long periods of time with their laptops making sure actual customers can't sit to enjoy their freshly purchased foodstuffs. Writing the next great American novel are you? Perhaps a groundbreaking screenplay? Reworking a presentation that will knock your client's socks off? Nine times out of ten…Candy Crush. Isn't it time for your nap in the park? Beat it, you filthy vagrant.

****

Not sure when or why it started but the handing out of party bags at kid parties: Whose birthday is it, anyway? Hey, why don't we give partygoers trophies as well to let them know how special they are for just showing up to a party where we are already feeding and entertaining them? Oh, and here's a medal for remembering to take your party bag home, Sparky!

****

The Mini Moo creamer: While I appreciate it when businesses aren't pushing that powdered creamer, they can certainly do better than the thimble-sized, for-some-reason-doesn't-need-to-be-refrigerated "cream." It takes about 10 minutes to shuck 35 Mini Moos just to get a decent color to my coffee. The world would be better served if they made a not-so-Mini Moo.

****

When government officials "call on" others in government to do something. That's what we're paying you for, to provide non-binding, passive-aggressive suggestions to people?

****

The self-appointed stewards of our social conscience who insist on inserting the knee-jerk "too soon" argument in response to provocative commentary or humor. We, the innocent and impressionable of society, thank you for your (copy & paste) service.

****

The TV Show "The Amazing Race" for propagating the ugly American stereotype. "Blah! Blah! Blah! Speak ENGLISH you sonofabitch and immediately drive us to the Sacred Pools! Just Go! Go! Go! Go!"

****

I hate "The Game" AND those who refer to themselves as "The Playa" (as in "The Player" ... I don't mind "La Playa" / The Beach)

****

Listicle websites: These are web lists or series of images, one-per-page, that you have to click through taking 100x-200x more time to view than if they were laid out properly on one page. Even if you can find the right "next" button on screen, the navigation rarely works reliably on mobile devices. Very clever, Mr. Marketing person. Now people will see a lot more ads and you'll improve some stupid site metric. [Web guy looking at web analytics funnel: "Oh wait, hundreds of thousands of visitors abandoned the site after just one click? What the?"]

****

The gelatinous, fat-like pockets found in cheaper deli meats, especially ham. I'm not sure if it's natural or as unnatural as the giant boneless meat fuselage surrounding it, but it creeps me out when my incisors rebound off of it. Whatever it is, I'm fairly certain headcheese is made entirely of it.

****

When grocery clerks/baggers decide which of your purchases go in a bag and which do not, without asking. "What about that milk?" "Oh, it's got a handle." "Yes but I have two bags that I can carry at the same time and one has room for the milk." Commence eye rolling routine to accompany the slow placing of milk into bag; Initiate incredulous look sequence as if I just rubbed my junk on the grocery scanner as my bags are dismissively slid to the end of the counter. Thank you, come again.

****

People, especially adults, spitting on the sidewalk or street. Unless you've just selflessly sucked venom from newbie snake charmer's leg, show some respect for yourself, for others and for this town we live in and use a napkin or swallow that loogie.

****

I still can't believe, in this digital day and age, that big, thick phone books are still delivered to our door. They are as wasteful and outdated as foreplay.

GRIEVANCES

****

Deadbeat Dog owners who walk around the neighborhood with no bags and therefore no intention of cleaning up after their little critter. [It's a "Call of Doodie" of sorts. Too much? Ah forget it, back to the rant.] When confronted they always deny that it was their dog that pooped on your property, as their dog is scooch-dragging its ass on your lawn in the background. I know it's every lawn owners fantasy to redeposit on a Dog Shit Denier's doorstep.

****

When mail says "Urgent...time sensitive...last notice" and the 'addressed to' includes "Or Current Resident." Yes, you get the finger. [Rip!]

****

Life is too short and precious to sit through any song by The Offspring.

****

When you are now first in line at a place like Starbucks and the person behind the counter shouts out, without making eye contact, "I'll help whoever's next." Uh, it's a line that you people organize with signage, ropes et al and I'm at the front of it – Who the hell do you think is next? Oh, so now you're absolving yourself of the responsibility to enforce international line protocols by announcing to everyone in the store that you really don't know who should be next? Really? Anarchy will ensue! Mayhem will reign supreme!! Welcome to ThunderDome, sir! Welcome to friggin' ThunderDome!!! [While all of this goes through my mind, the four people behind me in line have cautiously tip-toed ahead of me as I remain frozen in deep, angry thought.]

****

Low T: "If you're tired, lack muscle mass, can't fornicate for eight straight hours…you could have Low Testosterone." Yes, that must be it! We need MORE T as we get older, not less T! And now that I think about it, there IS a severe shortage of overly-aggressive elderly males in society. Soon bingo will be replaced by MMA at the retirement home.

****

As you enter the holiday season full of fancifully decorated cakes, cookies and houses of ginger, ask yourself the question that is on everyone's mind:
– "Who the hell likes the taste of marzipan?"
– "Objection: Rhetorical."
– "Withdrawn."

****

All songs these days are not just the artist, they are always "featuring" someone. "Beotch $lap" by Ke$ha featuring Pink, Will.I.Am, Wiz Khalifa, Biz Markie, Blake Shelton, Charo, Esteban, Caillou, Ruth Buzzi, Ann B. Davis, Morey Amsterdam, Rose Marie, Hugh Beaumont and Jerry Mathers as 'Da Beavah.' It may be a shorter to list who's not featured on the latest single. And if the song is a smash hit, they'd each only get $0.23.

****

Kids & Toothpaste: Kids have no problems zipping yogurt out of a GoGurt tube in 0.3 seconds but when it comes to toothpaste, they twist and strangle the damn tube like it owes them money. And the toothpaste gets everywhere except on their brushes. The medicine cabinet is filled with pasty stalactites and stalagmites that I need to spelunk through each day just to get to my brush.

****

The female preoccupation with shoes: I have a few pairs of shoes for utilitarian purposes but I have no desire to look at shoes in magazines and websites for hours on end. When questioned, the reversal. Her: "Well, a male dominated society forces women to wear high heels and bras and other instruments of conformity and torture to try to meet an unrealistic vision of beauty. My arches are in constant pain all because of you!" Him: "Huh? OK. By the power vested in me as a male representative of the species, I hereby release you from these misogynistic shackles." Her: "You men are always trying to control us! Don't tell me what to do. I'm going out." (Shopping for shoes, no doubt)

****

Movie theatre vending: Double the price of the already-expensive movie tickets. And then the upsell:
– "I'd like a small soda."
– "For only 34 cents more you can get a medium."
– "Ah, OK medium."
– "And for just 63 cents more for a large and 79 cents more for an extra-large."
– "Ah, do those come with a catheter and an insulin shot?"

****

Hotel bathroom signage that gives the line about not washing towels to save the environment: While it may be true I can't help thinking of the self-serving nature of said guilt trip as I snap a fresh towel under my nether regions, catch the other end behind me and start sawing like a goddamn lumberjack. Grab fresh towel and repeat. Hey, I'm saving the environment immediately around me.

****

Those crappy Facebook-targeted PlayBuzz quizzes: "Which invertebrate are you?" "Ha Ha! I got dung beetle...LOL!" Get the hell outta here.

****

The tendency toward hyper sensitivity and uber self-righteousness so prevalent in the world today. It's a race to see who can claim offense the fastest and then who can very publically put the "offender" in their place. So everyone can just stop putting their original thoughts and ideas out there so Tyler can feel warm and fuzzy in his little safe bubble and not have his delicate sensibilities accosted. Don't be so sensitive Tyler, you dopey cunt.

****

Movie theatre vending 2: "Would you like butter on your popcorn?" and you realize in hindsight she made subtle air quote motion as she said "butter." You quickly scan the signage as her words reverberate in your ears and you see in fine print a reference to ButtR™ and from that moment on you start questioning all reality as you unconsciously nod to the request and the ButtR™ starts glucking out of the dispenser, laminating your already-salted-and-flavored popcorn.

****

People who refer to their "personal brand." You're not Michael Jordan, jackass.

****

People like things to be black and white, as navigating the shades of gray is more nuanced and difficult. And in political correctness, nobody dare venture into the shade. "I've read that Hitler had a beautiful singing voice." "No! Hitler's singing voice was pure evil, you Nazi sympathizer!" "Perhaps you're right. But you have to admit...that Mussolini could play a mean shuffleboard!"

****

Animal crackers? That's bullshit, they're cookies.

***

Figure skating competitions: With all the soft, sappy music played during performances, all you need is a song with any kind of a beat that showmoms can clap to and you're on to the next round. Guaranteed. The skater doesn't even need to do any hard jumps. Just pump "Cotton Eyed Joe" though the speakers and speed near the boards with arms up in the air with an a huge, open-mouthed grin and the announcers will invariably say "Oh, she's working the crowd!" To seal the deal, the skater need only go to center ice, put hands on hips and kick each leg up and out in an exaggerated hoedown style dance and the place will go bonkers. Take that, Russian judge.

****

The kids in all Spielberg movies: Peppy and annoying. They are always smarter than adults, often pulling off the impossible like cracking into elaborate computer systems with a few keystrokes. I'm sure I'm not the only one who wanted the Goonies to get caught and the kids in Jurassic Park to get mauled by those velociraptors.

****

The Pita Chip: That winning taste & consistency combination of a stale fortune cookie and a tongue depressor.

****

When elected officials, especially members of Congress, say "THIS President" instead of "The President" as a way to distance themselves from the person, like "Oh, he's not MY President." It's disrespectful to not only the person and the office but also to the democratic process that put the President in office. And all sides do it when a President isn't of their party/persuasion. Election is over. Suck it up.

Fabric Softener Sheets: Why is it that you can lose a sock in the dryer on a regular basis but never lose those damn fabric softener sheets? In fact, it's the opposite: You put one sheet in with your laundry and like ten come out. And they attach themselves to your clothes like barnacles to a ship's hull. Even after you extract and dispose of them, they somehow crawl their way back. Used sheets are scattered all around my house and appear to be multiplying like goddamn tribbles.

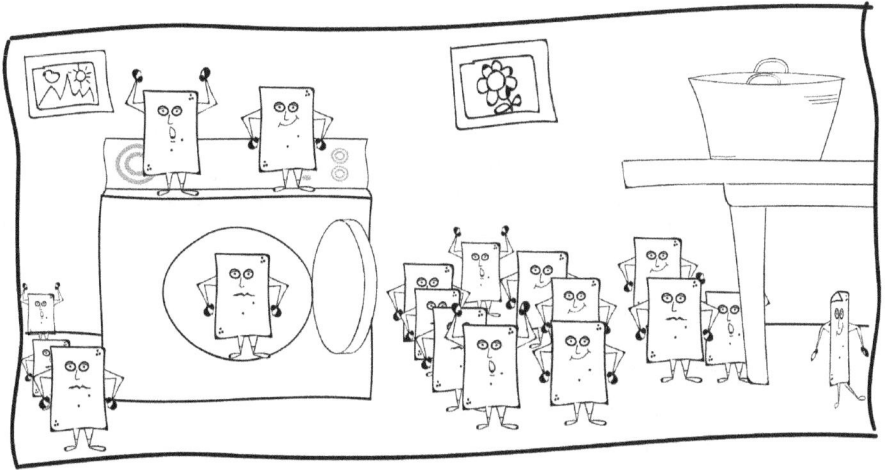

****

Restaurants, typically fast food varieties, that put restrictive openings on napkin dispensers so you can only fit the tip of your pinkies in, maybe, to get a tiny shred of a one napkin out. Some places hide the napkins altogether and dole one out with each meal. I only pretend to clean myself to keep up appearances so I'm not begging for more napkins, if that's the end game here.

****

Rock's unplugged movement: Yes, please cut the balls off of your music and try to sell it back to me. I really love hearing those strained acoustic guitar string bends during that solo. Hey, while you're at it, "break it down" even further into a Reggae version.

****

Dancing is Dumb.

****

The hyped videos that seem to be all over Facebook and other social sites with descriptions like: "Man comes face to face with a Grizzly Bear and what happens next is AMAZING!" You watch the whole thing and the end is never AMAZING. I'd love to see a similarly-titled video posted where the bear just mauls the guy as it would be AMAZING to see something on Facebook that actually happens in the real world.

****

Internet Trolls: These are people on the internet, hiding in anonymity, who pick fights on forums, chats and comment sections just for some sick pleasure. May they one day be ferreted out and confronted just to watch them recoil like the cowards they are. Maybe this Snowden character has the list of troll identities he can release...

****

The "Do Not Call" list seems to be a joke if not completely forgotten. While I'm sure some telemarketers could probably rationalize their cold call when pushed, like they have some tangential relationship with you already, there really should be an EASY and UNIVERSAL way to opt-out of any sales call without having to explain yourself to anyone. Something like "Press #86 at any time." My current "Go F*ck Yourself!" opt-out method is easy but not universally accepted, at least at the time of this writing.

****

One Way streets in downtown San Francisco: Not only numerous but change based on time of day, construction zones and phases of the moon. If you don't know what you're doing—and I'm a native so of course I don't—you could end up forced onto a bridge, unable to turn around as you're hopelessly barreling towards the Oregon border.

****

Use of the Oxford comma is often unnecessary, superfluous, and redundant.

****

LinkedIn: If you happen to cough while your LinkedIn profile page is open in edit mode, get ready for two solid weeks of "[yourname] has a new job! Say Congratulations!" followed with messages like "Congrats [yourname] on the new job! Hope all is well!!" from borderline acquaintances who wouldn't know any better. Most comments made by former colleagues on LinkedIn are pretty impersonal anyway and you'd think they were made by an algorithm and not actual humans. Even when someone is making a desperate plea for employment: "[yourname] is Currently Seeking new opportunities…I'll take anything!" followed by the comment "Hey, that's great! Take Care!"

****

The adult gummy vitamin: Have we become that soft of a society where we adults can't swallow a normal friggin' vitamin? Or at least grind it into a dissolvable powder? Doesn't everyone own a mortar and pestle? No? Oh, sorry.

****

The netting many clothing manufactures insist on putting into the typical male board short-style bathing suit. While for the average male it serves no actual purpose other than as a source of irritable chaffing, there is some understandable rationale for having a gathering function in the front...especially if you're looking to corner the 85-year-old-with-testicular-elephantiasis market. But why must the netting carry through to the back? Assuming most men possess sufficient control back there– not that a net would do much good if they didn't–the netting in the back serves merely for the promotion of itchy swamp ass. Surely we possess the technology to not have to go full panty.

****

PGA (Golf) propaganda, especially through First Tee commercials and Jimmy Roberts' fluff pieces, that proclaim that golf somehow teaches kids about dealing with life's challenges in the real world. If golf is life, I'm playing off the back tees with a hickory-shafted 1-Iron and gouged range balls into gale force winds.

****

When you slow to let a person move into your lane and they jerk in with fast motion like they're taking the spot by force. Of course, there is no conciliatory wave from Speed Racer afterwards. Bastard.

****

Pizza Rolls: Setting aside the not-as-good-as-they-should-be-yet-still-strangely-addictive taste and the oft-cited violent intestinal reactions to them, I believe pizza rolls were primarily engineered to maim. They come out of the oven or microwave retaining heat better than any known substance in the universe. I know this, with my years of intensive thermodynamics research of the snack food industry, but I still pop a barley-warm-to-the-touch roll into my mouth to then–only then–remember that it is actually filled with liquid hot magma. With eyes now dilated and watering, I employ an in-mouth juggling routine along with some crude circular breathing techniques and courageously press on (God forbid I now let them cool), shoveling more incendiary objects into my gob like white-hot coal into a steam train's firebox. The next morning there is scorched skin dangling down from the roof of my mouth like the stringy pulp from the inside of a freshly carved jack-o'-lantern. I understand that Totino's is working with the Department of Defense on fully weaponizing its Jalapeño Popper variety pizza roll.

****

Wine Stoppers: It's still a mystery what they're used for.

****

Chatty Experts on "Pawn Stars:" I'm sure the producers of the show encourage it but that makes it no less aggravating. Rick: "These Shroud of Turin washcloths are really cool but I don't know if they're real, so I'm going to call in someone to take a look at them." Expert arrives. Expert: "So Rick, what are your concerns?" Rick: "My concerns? Ah, the softening of the dollar against the Yen…tensions in the Ukraine… What the hell do you think my concerns are?! Are these washcloths authentic and what are they worth!?"

****

The flop: Sure, it happens in other sports but soccer is infamous for it. Yes, they are starting to penalize the act but there's nothing better than a cleat to flopper's nether regions as you shout "Now THAT'S a foul!" to prevent subsequent flop attempts.

****

Marketing speak, causing confusion and delay:

– Me: "In the last call you said you'd have the report done by now so we could review it in this meeting. Are you ready? "
– Marketing Guy: "Ah, that's quite an intriguing query regarding a most interesting paradigm. Let's put a pin in that, take it offline and I'll socialize that narrative with my colleagues on the morrow. Pending their time-sensitive feedback, we should be able to leverage synergies to gain traction on our core competencies and optimize our monetization strategy by our next meeting."
– Me: "So…you just forgot to do the report, right?"
– Marketing Guy: "That's right."

****

Use of the qualifier "arguably" in a discussion or argument: I guess it's used to concede that "one can certainly argue this statement but it's not my main point so let it slide for now" but I'm going to start using it aggressively in my everyday communications just to see what I can get away with:
– "The 1993 Sons of Boru, arguably the best Gaelic football team to ever exist, was the humblest team of them all."
– "My friend Jimmy Lucey, who is arguably more debonair than George Clooney, proceeded to clean the puke out of his clown suit."
– "While I'm arguably more erudite than Stephen Hawking, I don't know who Stephen Hawking is or what…means…erudite."

****

Petition people & fundraiser kids in front of stores: I live with enough guilt and I'm not looking for more. When I approach a store and see a table set up in front, and I absolutely must go in, I speed-walk my way up to "escape velocity." I barely make out the pitch to the unsuspecting retiree just ahead of me, something like: "Registered voter...save spotted owl...4 outta 5 dentists surveyed..." as I quickly work up my curt responses in an Eastern European accent "Me no vote...Owl taste good...What is dentist?" responses with my eyes trained on the ground just ahead of me. If I panic, I'm ready to invoke a stop, drop and roll getaway. I'm telling you business owners right now, if I drive up and see any of these shenanigans in front of your store I'm screeching away, rooster-tailing gravel up onto the side of your building and all those standing in front. That's right...you can kiss that $1.52 (mostly coins, with coupons) of sales goodbye!

***

Mall Aisle Vendors: These are the vagabonds who work in carts or pop-up structures that occupy the middle aisle of your local mall, selling God-knows-what. Often foreigners, they have the innate ability to catch your eye from 10 clicks away and subliminally lure you into their lair. ("Shit, I think I just floated over here like Wimpy smelling a hamburger!") They are always holding a neck pillow or petting some sort of potpourri snake...I don't f'ing know what they're holding because I'm always too afraid to look directly at their wares. "Ch-hello sir! Vood you like to feel...?" [cutting them off] "No! I'm good, thanks!" as I try desperately to break the hold of their gypsy tractor beam. I believe the really good mall aisle vendors graduate to be the barkers in front of the strip clubs on Broadway who force you to enter, night after night, and make you spend lots and lots of money against your will. The strip club barkers are a menace and there really ought to be a law.

****

Shopping Malls: I don't know what it is about shopping malls but it's obvious they were designed to drain the energy out of men and energize women. You see it in every mall: Women zipping from store to store at ever-increasing speeds and their male counterparts lagging behind, arms reaching out to their former partners, clutching nothing but air as they yell "Go on (cough)...go on without me...(cough, cough)" before they peel off to the electronics department of some store. I think malls ARE "The Matrix" where men are just oblivious batteries meandering around aimlessly, growing weaker with every step, as their energy is transferred in vast, invisible arcs to their wives/girlfriends. Some brave men enter The Mall Matrix with a purpose – Get in, Get what you need, Get out fast...like Morpheus – as The Agents (cologne sample peddlers, people taking dopey surveys and mall aisle vendors) desperately try to keep them from escaping. "When you see a mall aisle vendor, you do what we do. Run. You run your ass off."

****

The Microsoft Outlook email recall function: Doesn't seem to actually pull back sent emails but its attempted use will attract enough attention to increase the open rate of said emails by 1000%.

****

Hey, remember that time the guy driving the jacked-up truck with Oakland Raiders stickers & flags all over it let you safely lane change in front of him after you properly signaled? Nah, me neither.

****

Oil/Gas price fluctuations: The thin rationalizations made by "industry analysts" regarding these fluctuations are often more upsetting than the rising prices themselves. "Gas prices have spiked upon word that a Chevron refinery in El Segundo California was shut down yesterday for a few hours during their company picnic. The company has vowed to increase production to get volumes back up by sometime next Fall."

****

The phrase "Too much of xxx is a bad thing:" Of course, the phrase "Too much" denotes a limit has been exceeded so it doesn't matter what you add behind it, it's meant to be bad. "Too much love is a bad thing." Oh really? "Too much sex…" That's a myth.

****

When CEOs, politicians and other people in positions of power try to act casual and folksy to be more relatable to the average person. "Hey, look at Governor So-n-So with his sleeves rolled up, sitting with a beer next to that average joe with an uncomfortable look on his face – he's just like me!" I wouldn't elect anyone like me. And I prefer to dehumanize my superiors.

GRIEVANCES

****

Mobile devices at concerts: Not a quick shot or a short video but recording the whole damn thing, essentially watching a live concert through a screen of only a few inches. To what, post on a social media site later? What a waste. Proving that people today put more value in showing they were there rather than actually experiencing being there.

****

The powerful and clandestine Nutella lobby for convincing parents around the world that their sugary goop is somehow nutritious. "Oh, but it is made from hazelnut and cocoa!" Yes, and a Snickers is made from peanuts and cocoa and the first ingredient in both is sugar. "Start the day off right, Lil' Jimmy, and melt a Baby Ruth on that toast!"

****

Magazine Publishers for leaving page numbers off of random, non-ad pages to make you flip around to try to figure out where you are. Is it because the content on some pages is just so compelling that they didn't want to ruin it with a page number? Saving money on ink? Or is it so you flip around to find your place and you see more ads? Not sure but stop it already.

****

Waiting for someone to pull out of a parking spot: You try to be respectful and park a little further back and try not make eye contact, but have you ever seen such sloth-like behavior in your life? Sure, apply more makeup, you mime. Balance that checkbook. Finish knitting that sweater – I obviously have all day! Then the eventual "I'm not leaving" wave-off followed immediately with your involuntary, rage-induced thrusting of foot into and then down through the gas pedal floorboard to the pavement, and then the embarrassing foot-shuffling of your car away from the scene like Fred Flintstone.

****

CC cowards: People who always "Cc:" their boss on emails. It's the office equivalent of "I'm telling my Mommy!"

****

People, or organizations, who corner the concert purchasing market and buy all the tickets when sales open, only to hike the prices up for immediate resale. I'm not for waiting in lines again, but it did seem to be a fairer way to distribute tickets. Then again, I'm sure pro scalpers would just pay people to stand in lines, so I guess there's no way around it. So I'll just stay home...forever.

****

Commute calls from family or friends: You know, between 8a-9a or 5p-6p, when the person is obviously stuck in traffic and they want someone to be stuck with them, yet they have absolutely nothing to say. [Insert a half dozen "So, what else is going on?" utterances after awkward pauses that you hoped indicated the end of the call," here]. Gee, thanks for thinking of me. I'm a bit busy now but let me call you back at 3am when I have some insomnia time to kill.

****

The smarmy arrogance of luxury car commercials: "Let me give these jealous onlookers what they desperately need and drive by them so they can see this car again!" Hey, how about I take the giant bow from off the top of your car and strangle you with it? I'm sure I'd attract some jealous onlookers too.

****

Pseudo-Parenting by Facebook: "If I get 10000 likes my mom said I can get a nose job!" Best of luck, Brandi.

****

Businesses that tout that they are family owned: That's no selling point. I wouldn't do business with 99.999% of the families I know. No offense, you troglodytes.

****

Every time I ask my kids to pose for a photo they give a "tough" face and do some kind of pseudo-gang gesture, contorting their arms and/or hands. That's real street, ya punks. But for all I know it's a Mickey Mouse Club gesture. Is that even around anymore? [Pouring a 40 (Big Gulp) on ground] "...one for Funnachello."

****

That Fox NFL football robot that they show in the broadcast opening and at commercial breaks has a real attitude problem. Seriously. Total dick of an animated robot.

****

Those Personalization engines on websites these days make me even more myopic, which I didn't think was even possible. It's pretty interesting and all but it really skews one's perception of the world. For the longest time on Yahoo, I thought the whole nation was obsessed with news about the Golden State Warriors, Gravitational Waves and Auto-Erotic Asphyxiation. Ah, I'm just kidding, I added the middle one to try to sound smart.

****

When people, especially in-shape celebrities being interviewed, say "I love food." Oh really? I'm quite partial to oxygen myself.

****

Camping Tent Manufacturers that provide tent bags that barely fit their vacuum-sealed, machine-folded tents at the factory. As soon as you start to unzip your new purchase you instantly void the bag warranty as the tent blows out of the metal-toothed hole like goddamn jiffy pop. I'd pay an extra $40 for a baggier tent bag, just like I do for my slacks.

****

Credit/Debit Card readers, especially the ones at gas stations, that message you to insert and remove your card *quickly*. I don't know about you but each time I see that message, I take it as a challenge to my manhood. First, I roll up my sleeves and crouch with my feet shoulder-width apart at the optimal card-extraction height. I then insert the card with a confidence and precision of a top surgeon entering the funny bone cavity of the dude in the Operation game (Don't touch the sides!) and I immediately pull the card back like I'm yanking Excalibur from a goddamn stone. [Card Read Error] I'm sure the original readers caught the slow and steady card movement just fine but for some reason we built newer readers that can only read cards moving close to the speed of light.

****

When Rolling Stone calls their interview "[Person Name]: The Rolling Stone Interview." Oh, I thought you subbed that out to Mad Magazine. What happens when you interview that person again? Or is that the definitive interview, closing the book on that person forever? "[Person Name]: THE Rolling Stone Interview 2… This Time for Sure."

****

Customer v Self Service: When dealing with a business, like a bank, most people get all bent out of shape when they aren't helped by a real person. Not me. I'd much rather deal with a machine. I don't want to interact with anyone, especially some smarmy little shit wearing his first big boy suit staring at my bank account details from behind the teller counter. One time about 15 years ago I called my bank to get to the automated phone options and an actual person answered, so of course I hung up immediately. Now if someone would just invent the robotic dental hygienist already.

****

Blatant copycats: Lay's Stax are wannabe Pringles, only less tasty. Equal colored their sucralose packets to be the same as Splenda to trick people. Brilliant move, Marketing guy! Pleather is a total rip off of leather with an eerily similar name…I can go on and on and on.

****

The Prius seems like a capable car so you have to wonder if the Prius just attracts shitty drivers or if the car is just so difficult to drive that it turns adequate drivers into shitty ones. You'd swear these drivers just woke up from a 50-year coma and were immediately put behind the wheel of a Prius and sent on their way home from the hospital, with mouths agape and their wide-eyed surprise, observing the normal vehicular activity around them as they sluggishly occupy the fast lane. As a service to the driving public, Toyota should just apply student driver stickers to the backs of these vehicles as they leave the factory.

****

Web video ads that start on page load or when you happen to let your cursor go near them. You know, when I'm suddenly startled by loud music and over-the-top announcing, my instinct is not to drive my fist through the computer screen but rather it is to sit quietly and watch an ad for Tidy Cats.

****

The most overused phrases I've heard this year: "Life Hack," "Break the Internet" and "Get off me, you fat bastard!"

GRIEVANCES

****

Restaurant hosts/hostesses always give priority to a phone call over the people standing right in front of them. The phone rings and they react with as much urgency as someone trying to stomp on a burning fuse heading towards a stack of dynamite. Next time I'm in the back of the line waiting to meet the host, I'm going to screech out "RING! RING!" until I am escorted to the front of the line...or out of the building.

****

People waiting in line who are eating the food they are buying: Can't wait a few more seconds, tubby? Then the awkward presentation of the empty wrapper to the cashier: "Yes, I'd like to buy whatever...this... [handing empty wrapper]...was."

****

Suckered into watching a TED talk by its title and then a kid walks out onto the stage, dressed in hip clothes, wearing a sock cap with coiffed hair jetting out the front and starts to speak. I don't care if the little bastard cured cancer, I'm not watching it.

****

People who treat Facebook as slower, less accurate Google search: "Anyone know what time the Giants game is on tonight?" <crickets> <browser refresh> <elevator muzak loop> <browser refresh> </crickets>

****

Over-entitled pedestrians who don't slow down or even look when stepping off a curb, throwing glares at any vehicle that comes within 1000 feet of them in any direction of them. So sorry, you almost had to think about breaking stride as I drove past you on my green light. No, your sneer is certainly warranted. I'd like to accompany you on your first trip overseas [squash!]

****

When an item on a menu is described using the word "sustainable:" What the hell does that mean? I tried looking it up and nobody had a clear, legal definition of what that means as it pertains to food. "Excuse me waiter, what does it mean on the menu when you say the beef is sustainable?" "It means we sustain the economic viability of this restaurant when you buy it." "Ah, I thought so." I would think you'd be able to hike the price up if you claimed an item was "unsustainable." "This is it. Last batch. They ain't making any more of these stuffed White Rhino skins. Get 'em while you can!"

****

The timestamp function that video camera manufacturers in the '80s & '90s made sure turned on by default and actually burned onto tape so that we, and all future generations, could be constantly reminded of how stupid we were at that exact date-time for not noticing it while filming.

****

If your resume includes the terms "results-driven" and/or "visionary," we may be mortal enemies.

****

TV networks for milking successful series names/formats ad naseum, like "Law and Order" and "NCIS." The "CSI" franchise must be running out of spinoff ideas and title songs by The Who because I just saw a promo for "CSI: Colma" which opens to the tune "Boris the Spider."

****

Insultingly-transparent clickbait posts trying to goad you into action:
– "Facebook tried to ban this photo of an American eagle, cloaked in Old Glory, with guns in each talon protecting American babies from the Taliban. Like and Share this photo to show them …they'll never take …our freedom!"
– "Kim Kardashian said this highly decorated WWII Army Veteran (shown in this picture as a kind, elderly gentleman in an old-timey but tidy uniform) is a big, friggin' loser who should have died in the war. Don't let her and her wretched ilk get away with this! Like and Share this picture to put her in her place!!"
– And especially: Click HERE to purchase "Grievances" by Thomas McKeon!

The phantom jam: When there is a big traffic jam on the freeway and suddenly it opens up with no obvious reason for the slowdown, it's quite perplexing and also annoying. Now, I don't want to see remnants of major traffic accident–I don't wish harm on anyone–but give me something to explain the last 35 minutes of my life that I won't get back. Chickens escaped from a coop running all over the road with a farmer corralling them to the sound of guys playing the jaw harp and a whiskey jug. Or a Beauty Pageant bus overturned and contestants running all over the road being corralled by stranded motorists to the sounds of Mötley Crüe's "Girls, Girls, Girls." Give me something...

****

Submitting Online Job Applications: "Please upload your resume. Now type in all the contents of that resume into funky nonstandard form fields. We'll make sure some of the fields are mandatory but not marked as such, giving you errors when you try to submit. Error. Error. Error. Must specify salutation: Mr. Mrs. Miss. Ms. Dr. Prof. Rev. Other. Form submitted successfully. Thank you for wasting an hour of your time on our site just to make things easier for our hiring manager who won't look at your information anyway. You will never hear from us again."

****

The job interview response I wish I could take back: "Of course I have strong emotional intelligence! YOU'RE the one that doesn't have strong emotional intelligence, your big jerk!"

****

Pizza Hut pizza extremes: Cheese in crust. OK. Dips for pizza. Eh, a stretch but OK. Hotdogs baked into the pizza crust? Hotdogs. Hotdogs baked into the pizza crust. I think that was also the tipping point for Sodom and Gomorrah.

****

The forced pleasantries from the pilot and flight attendant at the plane door when your deboarding: "Bye. Buh Bye. Bye Now. Take Care. Take Care Now." What do you say to them? "Good flying, Ace…thanks for not killing us all." "Man, those peanuts you sold me really hit the spot!" The whole forced interaction makes me want to jump out the back of the plane and onto tarmac, taking my chances dodging planes and Homeland Security. I'm sure it's the worst part of their jobs so just end the practice.

****

Jam, not jelly. Jelly gets the finger.

****

When you beat another driver to a four way stop and he gives the "Mr. Cool Guy" look away and with the exaggerated yet dismissive motion of the fingers, giving you permission to go. "Lord Commander, Ruler of the Roadways, I thank you for your compassion and leniency. I am but a humble vagabond trying to find my way and am not worthy of such kindness. By your good graces I must take leave of you now, but know that I shall labor to not meet your benevolent eyes as I cross your hallowed path. May eternal blessings and good fortune follow his Lordship all the days of his life."

****

Barf bags on airplanes: First off, why are they so small? Considering their purpose, and the potential for collateral damage, you'd think they'd be as large as possible. Secondly, the bags are a little too difficult to open and expand quickly for such an urgent and volatile delivery. Planes should be equipped with a barf button that when pressed causes a protective bubble to explode out of the seat in front of you, like a car airbag, surrounding you on all sides. Toto would make a model of the barf airbag that has robotic arms that would quickly take your temperature, shoot a Dramamine pill into your mouth, wash and dry your face and comb your hair before releasing you back into a cabin of unsuspecting passengers. These could also come in handy in some of the dive bars…I read about.

****

Those people who get up as soon as plane lands so they can get just a few rows ahead while everyone else waits patiently to file out in a logical and civilized manner. And you know most of these "premature evacuators" aren't rushing to catch another flight. They're probably the same a-holes who pull into a merge lane and drive down to the very end and cut back over. And "in the event of a water landing," you know these bastards will claw over you to get the raft and once safely aboard will push off. They must be stopped before it's too late.

****

Guys who jack their trucks up but do not realign their headlights. What, you think the people in front of you flipping you off are just jealous of your killer rig, Hoss?

****

"Wooo!" People: When you're in a crowd–at a club, sporting event or especially at a concert that is being recorded for a live album while the singer is talking to the crowd, and you want some attention but you don't have anything actually useful to offer, just yell "Wooo!" at the top of your lungs and at random intervals. *Bonus attention points if you also raise your arms over your head while howling the aforementioned "Wooo!"

****

The sweater vest and vest jacket: I've never understood the rationale of "warming the core" when it's your extremities that get cold and drop off with frost bite. Actually, I could see buying only the arms of the jacket before buying a vest jacket. I think they had that concept in the 80s for girl's legs, called leg warmers. I actually couldn't tell if the leg warmers were detached on each leg or if they were a connected to some fuzzy britches because girls' midsections were typically obscured by those big, long, form-hiding sweaters back in the day. Man, it must have been a lot colder back then.

****

Pinterest: I'm still not sure of its purpose and I'm convinced nobody else knows either. What if it was revealed that the only purpose of Pinterest was to keep women busy so the boys could go to the pub? I think I'd get in on that IPO.

****

"No War For Oil" bumper stickers on gas powered vehicles

****

Has anyone else watched an entire song by the Lady Birds on Benny Hill waiting for the slapstick punchline that never came? That was some nepotistic bullshit right there, Benny.

****

Voicemail: People who still insist on giving verbose instructions on how to leave a message. Save some natives who have just received a Coke bottle from the gods, the rest of humanity now understands how to leave a message so there is no need for the lengthy lesson:

– "Hello Saul…It's Murray. Hello? Hello? Huh, that's Saul's voice but it sounds like a recording of some kind. What's that you say? Leave your name, eh? (Scribbling) And your number, you say? (Scribbling) And what? The time you called and you'll get back to me?" (Scribbling)

– "Murray, who are you talking to on the phone?"

– "The future, Blanche. The FUTURE!"

****

Thank you, Conference Call Attendee, for not realizing you are *not* on mute as you type incessantly, making everyone else on the phone endure the barrage of keyboard clatter and ruining the meeting. And you are oh so important, typing away, as you obviously don't need to listen to the discussion in which you were invited to participate. I really look forward to the awkward pause and your generic if not ill-fitting response when someone asks you a direct question during the call, followed by the eventual "ah, can you repeat that?" admission.

****

"The Book was Better" people: You know, when talking about a movie adaptation of a book: Some people are always compelled to throw that in before describing the movie, which you're barely interested in anyway. Well, look at you. Aren't you the avid reading genius? I'll bet the books you read don't even have pictures! Books have too much filler so to them I say: "The CliffsNotes were Better"

****

Back in grammar school, giving someone "cuts" in line might raise a few eyebrows but was a generally accepted practice in most kid circles throughout the civilized world. But the controversial "back cut" was the modern day equivalent of taking your glove off and slapping the original person behind you right across the goddamn face. For this very reason, I have a very long payback list. But, patience. Patience.

****

I'm no lawyer but the "We reserve the right to refuse service to anyone" sign seems to grant store owners tremendous powers of discrimination. If you were a potential patron of ill repute and you removed the sign when the merchant's back was turned, could you then invoke an unchallenged, inalienable right to be served? Merchant: "Oh, I don't think so, you filthy vagabond! [Thrusting arm with pointed finger towards a clean, greaseless square of original paint on the wall]. What the...??" As the smiling street urchin, now removing his shirt and shoes, barks out his food order.

****

When my wife goes out of town with friends for the weekend there is always a "honey-do" list left behind for me: "Get the kids haircuts...each kid has to be in different places at the same time...vacuum all the rooms...go grocery shopping at 3 different stores because my list contains items only found in specific stores...clean all the toilets...darn the socks I left on the table...clean the chimney...paint the fence – Up! Down! Side to Side!" If I tried to hand her a list of things to do when I was headed off for a guy's golf weekend she'd pull my heart out like the witch doctor dude in *Indiana Jones and the Temple of Doom*.

****

There must be a class in graduate school that teaches students how to awkwardly work into casual conversation the fact that they actually went to grad school.
– "I'll never forget the morning of 9/11...as it was exactly 2 years, 3 months and 12 days since I finished grad school."
– "You know, I did a lot if thinking about the meaning of life and of love and of loss...back when I was in grad school. So anyway, sorry to hear about your mother's passing this morning."
– "Bless me father for I have sinned. It's been 8 months since my last confession... back when I was in grad school."

****

Seats on bicycles, like touring bikes: They are a little too form fitting to one's crevasses for any non-eunuch's comfort, forcing the purchase of special pants with padding. Perhaps the padded pant makers are in collusion with seat manufactures? Last time I went for a ride I had to keep checking to make sure the seat was still on there and that I was not stuck onto the seat post. The seat shape can't be an aerodynamics issue since most asses more than amply cover them so perhaps it's a bike weight issue? If it is a weight issue I'd go without handlebars in favor of a nice comfy seat. I wonder if you can get these refitted with that banana seat from the 70s? Bicyclists and shop owners all say that your backside will get used to it, which should be noted is also part of a warden's speech to new inmates.

****

The Catholic church has a long history of "leveraging" ancient traditions & ceremonies for their own religious holidays but some of it comes off as a bit transparent nowadays. "This Thursday is of course July 4th which is one of the most blessed days in The Church, the feast of St. Theodore of Cyrene. We'll be having special masses throughout the day and we trust you will join us." Ah, nice try Monsignor.

****

Marketing folks who attempt to invent a technical term for their product by merely inserting the word "technology" to the end of a generic, often very-literal phrase. "The 2017 Toyota Camry uses 'advanced car stopping technology' to keep drivers safe." "The new Tide uses 'shit stain removal technology' to remove even the toughest man marks."

****

Websites that pop a 'Don't leave!' message when it detects your mouse going to the browser navigation. I have enough people telling me what to do, thank you very much.

****

Commercials where drivers/cars are performing outrageous and completely CGI'd stunts and you see the legal disclaimer come on the screen "Professional driver...Closed course...Do not attempt." "Now if I could just get my F150 strapped to the nose of a Saturn V rocket I bet you I could...oh wait, there's a legal disclaimer. Damnit!"

****

The CPAP Sleep Apnea Device: Their slogan should be "The CPAP Mask: Because your chance of gettin' some isn't slim enough already."

****

My kids are at an age when they seem to wear clothes only for a couple of hours and then they toss them into the laundry and put on the next pair of shorts, pants or shirt. What's with constant wardrobe changes there, David Lee Roth? They need to learn to do what I do which is to always start with the same outfit as the day before and only change it if the likelihood of seeing the same non-relative two days in a row exceeds 79%. Voila.

****

Mother's Day is the day your wife gets a break from you and the kids, goes to a spa, gets her nails done and enjoys cocktails with friends as she thinks about what tweaks she still needs to make to you. Father's Day is the day your wife says you spend with family.

****

I'm not one who should be giving relationship advice but if "Every Kiss Begins with Kay" (jewelers) then maybe she's not that into you.

www.ingramcontent.com/pod-product-compliance
Lightning Source LLC
LaVergne TN
LVHW091157080426
835509LV00006B/723

9780999824490 7